ARRANGING THE BLAZE

ANHINGA PRESS

Cover art: *Drain 3,* resin and spray paint on wood by Melissa Hutton
Author photograph: Jennifer K. Sweeney
Typesetting, production, and cover design: C.L. Knight
Type Styles: titles set in Bernhard Modern Standard;
            text in Adobe Garamond Pro

Library of Congress Cataloging-in-Publication Data
Arranging the Blaze by Chad Sweeney – First Edition
ISBN – 978-1-934695-09-8
Library of Congress Cataloging Card Number – 2008931769

This publication is sponsored in part by a grant
from the Florida Department of State,
Division of Cultural Affairs, and the Florida Arts Council.

Anhinga Press Inc. is a nonprofit corporation dedicated wholly to the
publication and appreciation of fine poetry and other literary genres.

For personal orders, catalogs
and information write to:
Anhinga Press
P.O. Box 10595
Tallahassee, Florida 32302
Web site: www.anhinga.org
E-mail: info@anhinga.org

Published in the United States
by Anhinga Press
Tallahassee, Florida
First Edition, 2009

for Jennifer
Mom, Dad and Andrea

CONTENTS

BASHO'S ROBES

ARC OF INTENTION

ACKNOWLEDGMENTS

Grateful acknowledgments to the editors of the following publications in which these poems first appeared, sometimes in different forms.

Barrow Street: "California"

Bellingham Review: "City Pastoral"

Blueline: "Climax"

Cimarron Review: "The River"

Coconut: "33 Translations of One Basho"

DMQ Review: "Fire Escape as Axis Mundi" and "The Inheritance"

Electronic Poetry Review: "Notes Toward Making"

Forklift, Ohio: "Dolores Park"

Hunger Mountain: "Composition"

Mirage #4 Period(ical): "The Welders" and "The Concrete"

Nimrod: "The Osprey"

Packingtown Review: "White"

Parthenon West Review: "Genealogy"

Passages North: "The Mile" and "Translation"

Puerto del Sol: "The Navajo Poet"

Runes: "Arranging the Blaze"

Santa Clara Review: "Bear"

Tea Party: "Oklahoma"

Transfer: "History" and "Kochanek"

Throwback Magazine: "Methodist" and "The Witness"

Jump (Anthology, WritersCorps Books): "The Arc of Intention"

A few poems appeared in the chapbook: *Nail By Nail the Sunlight* (Urban Iris Press, Brooklyn 2003). "Is" and "Night" appeared in a film exhibit by Artist/Film Maker Eric Zener in the Hespe Gallery of San Francisco in the Spring of 2005. A part of the poem, "Night" appeared as section 42 in *An Architecture* (BlazeVOX, 2007).

A deep bow of gratitude to my teachers and readers for their input and inspiration: Paul Hoover, David Holler, Jennifer Kochanek Sweeney, Maurice Kenny, Maxine Chernoff, Roxane Beth Johnson, Jason Morris, Zaid Shlah, Stacy Doris, Susan Gevirtz, and Toni Mirosevich.

ARRANGING THE BLAZE

THE RIVER

I went to the river and watched a house burning
noiselessly, cattle birds

remained asleep on the roof.
I went to the river and the wind shook me

but did not shake the pears
from the branches.

I went to the river and found a desert
rising gradually toward the Pleiades,

lions panted beside a boat
half-buried in red sand.

I went to the river and the churches had fallen,
library books swirled away in the flood

their pages turning slowly
as if someone in the water

were reading them.
I went to the river and jumped

from my little bridge
in the tuxedo I wore to the wedding

pockets full of rocks and old
foreign coins. I went to the river

and saw vines sprawling
over the columns and steps

of the Capitol.
Children were born beneath wild

flowering trees. Some died,
but most of them lived.

GENEALOGY

The bones are scattered
but don't wait to be found.

They sing from where they are.

WHITE

Not a simple question.
The foam of the sea is white,

gypsum scowling the hillside,
the sun-bleached bones of crows.

White is neither yes nor no.
Look at this cat blinking sleepily.

Neither absence nor presence.
Look at the rim of your thumbnail.

White cares nothing for purity
but will stand guard at the graveyard

with its library of stone books,
moon with its hooks in the tide.

White is not kind.
Look at the cotton opening its seed.

GENEALOGY

Along the streets
the candelabra
in amber points of sun

reflected,
car glass, arc-of-roof, antenna.
It is in me.

The eye of a raven
against fields of snow,
the raven itself a kind of eye,

the roving eye of winter
by which the winter
watches itself,

from shifting angles, caught
in a flurry, now anchored
briefly to pine—by memory

or dream,
I don't know how it arrived.
It is in me.

Mother before she was my mother,
Sherryl hung
by her knees from the redbud tree,

allowing the white Sunday
dress to flow over her head,
allowing

her hair scented with lye and faith
to comb patterns in the dust,
recording the day upside down:

the smart white house of Mary's father,
who emerged in his Sabbath black to cast
a look of such contempt

and hurry his daughters into the car—*No,
Sherryl can't come to our church anymore*—
that the moment of the first shame

would evoke itself
in a thousand carpeted hours.
It is in me.

A cypress throws its windy shape
against night, a portrait begun the first clock
lightning struck the water, a portrait

over which the cypress agonized since before
it was seed. A painting stars drafted,
sea memorized. Color of a gull's

hunger. Color of rainbow before the rain
let go from its cloud.
Color roots spoke to turtle eggs.

Is it jade? Is it flint?
Did waves grind it
in a mill? It is in me.

Knuckle
bloody against the plow.
Grandpa Sweeney fell when no one

was looking, the last hawk
in the net of his eye
recorded briefly in the ash.

My father
leapt down from that tractor
to bury his own

boyhood, eleven years old and Irish,
fatherless, godless, barefooted boy,
stricken among the wheat

which by its very shape
reflected millennia
of locust and gestured that it too

had measured the voices
of creek and coyotes
sleeping in fence rows. Knuckle

against the plow, a thorn bush
planted that day
in my father's eye. It is in me.

And the first hand to blend
pollen and clay against the cave wall,
mother

of Lilith,
Harjo and Levertov,
mother of jasmine clutching at cliff ledge,

mother of a drizzle one
particular day settled down
over the rooftops of Dresden

to reappear
centuries later as a stand
of aspen along a glacial brook.

By memory or dream
it arrived.
It is in me.

HISTORY

It happened slowly
the way cliffs raise the bones of whales.

When I opened my mouth to sing
darkness swarmed out redolent

of diesel,
a Buick struggled to wake in snow.

My mouth was not a mouth
but a wound grown old

beneath the rails of tin mines,
a wolf

constellated of Northern Lights
revolved like an engine in the sky.

My teeth stood in a ring of idols—
bison, bear, raccoon—

recalling the flavor of rain
licked from a willow root.

THE NAVAJO POET

for Sherwin Bitsui

He spoke from the back room of a storm
where sky fires revolved around a ship's mast.

The Golden Fleece was a thing made of words,
the wool a man grows

to warm himself in the blue snow
of desert mesa. Nations disappeared

in search of this cloth,
crows belled from the eaves

rang only for the guilty. Even their shadows
left fingerprints along our vertebrae.

Corner stores staggered to *Route 66*
to thumb a ride from the ghosts of coyotes

in gravel trucks. Citizens
pinched money between their eyelids

like the drying hands of butchers—
the bonesaw rattled with bridges.

A shepherd sang from far away,
a lizard born of solar wind

crept inside the well of a cactus to sleep.
Beggars founded their own city

in the long median that burns with oleander
from Miami to L.A.

The beer tasted of uranium.
Flint Wing auctioned the Milky Way's pelt

for a dawn-streaked Pontiac
with a full tank of gas.

BEAR

for Maurice Kenny

Monday on the way to work
I must have taken a wrong turn.
Bougainvillea climbed the doors,

an unfamiliar alley
in the silence of trees.
The bear rose before me

in a cloud of fur,
roared
in every language at once.

I threw the dictionary at him.
I threw my calculator at him,
the keys in my pockets, my credit cards.

I threw the Bhagavad Gita, its pages dog-eared,
the Constitution, the original,
all Rilke's letters.

I threw the Cabala at the bear,
My God!
   I shouted.

The bear's shadow grew all around me.

THE WELDERS

Black Rock Desert, Nevada

I watch the welders make the carousel,
angular on one knee, atop a ladder,
amidst flame and their own private cloud

of dust or smoke
or something else, like memory—
adjoining beams at right angles,

the joists, the wheels,
one tongue of fire
like a word.

Under the masks
they are magicians
seaming sky

to mountain
with a red stitch,
a green stitch.

I've seen their work before,
wherever theory
or bone

needed binding,
would otherwise lie back
in its own vein of ore,

iron
among malachite,
Irish among their dead,

scars beneath the breasts
where the coal train crosses.
Civilization

depends on this,
this math
at the wrist, at the mouth.

The welders are laughing now
above their heavy
boots, holding the cold beer

against the vein in their neck.
The carousel is turning.
It's night! The dragons!

TUNISIA

for Michael and Philip

Weekends we can go to Karawan,
he says, *a caravan town*
where the Arabs who occupied Spain

retreated to build
this severe Moorish architecture ...
but I don't know how they'll feel

about two Men living together—
while over his left shoulder
I'm watching a hummingbird

tread the air in
delight
of the fuchsia flutes—

purple, no,
red—
grown up

from the ground and bowing.
The man's
voice

a vibration
at midday,
a phenomenon of wind and blood:

the story hovers
in the far
            hope

16

or fear,
which
is it?—the demure

blooms
in dappled suspension
or that shimmer of wet jade

we interpret as wings?

TRANSLATION

for Palestine and Israel

Run your tongue over your teeth.
Tell me these are not bones

of the leviathan,
the blind wood

of shipwrecks.
Tell me this is not an alphabet,

a necklace of keys.
This wind—

this long wind from the sun
looses the doors from their moorings

and carves in the olive grove
a boy, a violin without strings.

Run your tongue over your teeth.
Tell me this is not the glass

of fallen houses.
Tell me this valley

has forgotten the snow
on its white stem.

Claim.
Moon lies down beside the arrowhead.

Claim.
Blue clouds billow from rock.

Run your tongue over its reef.
This is your name, your cypress bough,

and the sea is on fire—
the only.

MOVING

This truck drags the road beneath us.
By turning the wheel I swing
the mountains

into the rearview mirror.
Words are everything
we own.

When my cockatiel escaped
into the snow,
I assumed he was confused

and would choose,
if given the choice,
not to freeze.

Little yellow comet!
He knew
what he was doing. Let

our marriage be like that.
Let windows
stay open

to distance. What goes
the rain will bring.
Palm fronds

in our kitchen.
Love is love in
leaving.

CITY PASTORAL

the bull

cut at birth
for our ease   his wet eyes

take in the field
the one sprawled oak holding

the hill
arranges the blaze

around it

a green heart pumping above
the platinum

grass of late summer   not color
to the grass   a feeling

of dryness   or
purpose   not for me

to redeem what
has survived perfectly

against the storefront and under
blankets her feet just

sticking out   her red feet
we step around and into

the antique shop to buy
a license plate and someone's

mother
framed among lamps

the heart in its night   crosses
the current toward

an island   I've seen it
in the black water

the bull no longer bull   what
name then   working his way up

the hill
that sound   can you

hear it   when his teeth pull
at the grass

ARRANGING THE BLAZE

Into the eye the light pours
              of red brick and black brick and wire draped
                    against white, opaque white a surface
                            of distance the
                                    irreconcilable,
of gables and doors, of the impressions of pedestrians stooped
through rain, to the blur of
the water tower over roof peaks in muted triangles.
And somewhere: there: the contours of sound
                      those tires now on wet
                      pavement, and there
                      a plane
                      in the pearl, the milk bruise,
                      how to say it, of sky—sounded—and
                  where do *I* end?

This oxygen now
by which my body burns arrived from
over the sea while I
slept all night. A great invisible
wing
dragged its mass over the water—while ships
                          while darkness
                          while strangers in cars
                  while cliffs while pine while elevators and
jail beds—while tides
combed the
reef and
                  lobsters moved in the living rock—

this air
poised on its axis in

time—the water, the water

in my body   waving.

Gingko trees flare yellow
out of memory, still spark
the eye. The beach grass
                    must be where I left it
                              wrapping
the whole earth last year,

how old is it
beside the sea—to be still
making me with its arc,
its sand, its small portion
of space worn about it like a shawl?—*tremolo*
in blue-green radial symmetries
of the beach grass.

Block upon block the buildings
scrape against
                    hills, mounting to where eucalyptus
claim the peaks—those lights
in houses, someone chose them, and by their blaze
against this water I am also lit. Over the empty

playground in diagonals of rain, the flock
throws itself into storm, buoys
and pivots—a wind of swallows

directed from within,

        churns above the city

     —and is this Lebanese cedar,

center point,

     abandoned and returned toward, part

     of the flock?

        And the shingles part?

that barge docking?

the feeling too—of joy—a thing

           in our gravity

       over which this net of eyes casts,

    the one and the many

      —and you

   who see it, shifting—?

OF MEMORY AND INNOVATION

―――――――――――

THE WITNESS

for Mary Ruefle

Any moment now the day will begin.

Hedges guard their quarry of night.
An immense door is rocking.

Who else but me to say it?

Then something hesitates.
The rooftops send up

their birds.
I'm terrified

by how much I love.

THE OSPREY

Fog makes it easier to believe.
Wet, gangly trees

slope up from the water
bluegreen and graygreen

in half-written stanzas
disappearing by degrees,

the sun an idea only
where beach plums ripen

in the sky first
then on the branch,

seagrass saying *Wind*
saying *I* and *Thou*

and the osprey—
no more holy

than the water rat or cormorant
or beached kelp glistening

from last night's tempest—
no less holy

than the wood in this bench
than the stone in this man,

the kingdom of the small
overwhelming the kingdom of the large—

from this and into this
the osprey breaks

with a fish in its talons—
and here is the world:

an osprey bearing a fish
and the word *fish*

over power lines and marsh crabs
above swans and rotted docks

up to the platform on the utility pole
flapping three more times

to the shapes of hunger in the nest.

CUL-DE-SAC

Here the broken
window
no one bothered to replace.

Here the swing set
over-vined
with jasmine,

a tricycle
rusting,
all manner of desire.

Nowhere else
this rat
unafraid among weeds,

the grass become wheat
sun-dried and immortal.
And a dark-haired child,

a new thing among the worlds,
broods over a baby snake,
its emerald head

turning
under the jelly jar,
its living eyes.

METHODIST

My knees could barely hold to the end
of prayer. Candles blurred to a hymn
of bees among lemon boughs, sun

illumined dust in its fractured beams.
Of the voice I understood
the rhythm only, or maybe

the shape: a bellows
loved and demanded,
vowels falling from the mouth

of the cross.
I watched the old and tried on
their faces. Like stone boats.

     Heaven
was a blue suit, I thought,
a row of elbows in haunted light.

Still, at times
something happened
like waking suddenly

in a larger dark,
surrounded
by the fish's belly.

OKLAHOMA

The wind smelled of grass fires
and carnival horses and oil.
Wind was the only calendar.
Alfalfa wind. Cotton wind.

The stadium lights shut off
but someone lit a cigarette
and the game continued.
The whirring of the ball was enough.

I watched a swath of darkness
where the crowd must have been,
a trench in the air. I cried
to be taken home to our canyon.

Grandmother had a few gray
feathers growing from her neck.
I touched them while she slept
which enabled me to read

the wind as if it were braille.
Ghost wind. Cherokee wind.
There were owls in cages
appearing and disappearing

through doors my sister and I
failed to understand.
Grandma was afraid of snakes
but nothing else. She killed

rabbits with her bare hands.
Her voice drew a line between us
which trembled
like the surface of a story.

COMPOSITION

Wire fence and thistle beyond,
hose in loose coil, shovel left out—

smoothed and mounded under one snow.

Beside the frozen gate
whirled from a stillpoint
                            the cedar tree
        what suddenly the sky made
        in whiteness

                            three
                            red
                            birds.

It was too early for the eye.
It was the first winter morning

caught the boy alone
in the dark house—
the chosen branch shook

a little
and the cardinals watched him
through the window.

The boy thought they were far older
than birds,

the map of broken things
composed

around them,

the white made vast
by that small blood—

and something flew out from him
over the fence,

over the field.

THE CONCRETE

There were no sailboats that day.
It was land and only land.

No unrealized possibilities
hobbled along the sidewalks

or stood trembling in December leaves.
No windows from which gray whales

surfaced. No orchids, no bells.
Only a garden hose left on,

a woman
asleep on the stairs, a yellow

bathrobe
hung from a thorn bush, and a shoe.

And wind and not wind
moving along together

through doorways and halls,
threading up the chimney a pale

ash, that house on the hill
dreamed of but never built.

THE GREAT POEMS

There is a fat man
      in a palanquin
I carry.
           The man is me
and I carry him.

He doesn't look to the side
      or down
but straight ahead to the road's
          turn
and I carry him.

He takes what he wants
      from the market—
oranges the old men balance in pyramids,
          flaming birds in cages
and I carry him.

The great poems of the earth
      are written by the earth
in leaf and hoof and birth.
          The king is jealous of what he loves
and I carry him.

IS

to make my body a castle is
supple as the water is
through the reeds the watersnake leaves
the long alphabet is

the is that wills and tumbles is
the is that billows egrets is
the is that winters iron is
the is that drags the rain uphill

the loam invites the midnight is
the boat afloat on fire is
the stone its own wet shelter is
the door that aprils wheat

to make my body a violin
trembling with the spider's mouth
a music thin enough to snow
the is that burns inside the now

FIRE ESCAPE AS AXIS MUNDI

A guitar queries the fire escape
a hundred stories above

and cigarette embers drift down
like search lights,

nostalgic and prophetic,
the dna of a century,

falling into the past
and future equally

falling from a place beyond both,
and everywhere the bent pale

flowers, all ruffled and wrong
and Jacob's angels de-

scending the clotheslines into Harlem,
sky below and death above,

a little spiral wind of
kitchen smoke—

then someone laughs into the invisible,
a thief stops to touch

the glass mouth of a mannequin,
no moon but gravity's

helix—and night
welded to its corner beams,

sweet meaningless night,
reliquary for the irrational

to whom I address my prayer.

NIGHT

what clothes tomorrow will be worn
how many millions   and who
chosen

alone   and in waves
make history

what words this hour unborn
flock out toward love in elevator light

when the unbroken air
anchors moon in its window

before anyone's left town
before the betrayal

when the fire is folded inside its wood

night when the animals
night when the tunnel

when diamonds lie unfound in the rock

when Valencia
        is hung of oranges   in luminous ice

your face   asleep in our bed
                is watching   something

I can't possibly know what

DOLORES PARK

San Francisco

In time-flow the changing and changeless:
shadows even move when the wind moves
against the curves of land and city:
magnolia, cypress, palm:

                    stand

vertical in mind as citizens
of the forest in overalls, bored and waiting for a bus,
mumbling into a past, a shovel, a fire, remember this, tree:
as equivalent to a man, a
king, a witch, a mother

        in the vegetal: remember this: and: and:

        intone with every atom their shape, the arc
of reach and surrender, the dwarfish trunks, and bark
of whirled lexicon: of years: resolute in rings: the parrots:
small green shadows authored by jungle,
fashion nests out of distance
bits of twisted spring and ribbon—

           Dolores Street leaps from its map a living thing
        crossed, reclined, alert or livid eye,
leading Tierra del Fuego to New York, barefoot and tired,
Old Man Road—

The park rumples a patterned rug
              in swift descent from mountain to surf
one rectangle of mind over-
         lapped, mumbling in sleep
         its polyphone of root and petal, its chorus of secret
word and public word

in grass grown soft but not to itself soft
soft only to the woman supine in office clothes mutejoydown
and soft to the lovers lying close and naked despite their clothes
and soft to the carpenter who rests carbuncular in dreamsmile beside
                              his hammer
and soft to the shadow of clouds without syntax clean and empty of
                              water
and soft to the eye sweeping over and fixing on *that* and *that* and *that*
          pixelated electric meadow of the eye sun-wheeled and burning
and soft to the dead who lie in memory murmuring love among bees
and soft to the summer child I was, fallen from the bike and reborn
and soft to the hips of Ruth and Bill and Drake bundled
                    into a communal whiskey stupor
but to itself is grass only, material and sharp
(the dandelion whose beauty
              is body, and deadly serious against the millennia)
dreaming in the language of grass: of shape and desire, a pregnant
absence
              and we
              think and are thought

by this city, our form entire (bridge, girder, lake)
billows to the shape of vision as far as
              the windows of Oakland, ships and docks
the pine hills in retrograde blue distance, and back
into the small
                    years: shape and desire: for every
                              leaf: mind!

A child launches from the swing into sand, lands badly and wails
in the same language all over the world. Shoes make good
spades to dig and fill a hole, to bury the foot and giggle
while on the platform above, the brother plans an attack: shape
of play and leaf the same, each in its own flesh,

                    rib
              of memory and innovation

fur

root

a green

rain

            the palm trees toe their hill
and now and now: and: and: now is: and: and memory tree
and material tree: each of a weight:
and the church tower says forever above the butterflies
and the street erupts from ideal and real equally
and cars grind up the hill against the chains
and the squirrels balance the slack geometries of wire
and time mends its clock in the wings of a fly, a universe
turning at those wings, little

                  sphinx panting,
                  pterodactyl of the afternoon,
made thing, gold thing, green-gold and diamond eye
ornately hung against this hour:
reveal, disrobe

        your world within the doll:

                  my thief
                  my seed

           my obsidian

                        my sapling
                        my siege
                                my cardinal inventing snow
                                my piano
                                my century
                                my sin
a ripple on the fabric to denote wind:
wind over city and mind the same: gust and the colors run
                                the net lowered into space yawns
and the forms and fish caught there
shake a little like the shaking of worlds.

After work, the hour of dogs:
a beagle hunts the tennis ball with original glee,
all else dim beyond that wet star:
life as composition in drafts, approximations, each
dog resembles its man, its woman, in face and soul,
thirteen roll naked there
                sniffing and licking under the green day:
        and I, the fourteenth, in word
        in ecstasy of word only, and clothed, withdrawn, shy
        a maker
        of word only
saunter past with hands in pockets
to rest in the shade of palms again and know the city
in weightless ideal
                in line and dome
                        like history to the safe,
soft as thistledown,
                the bombs falling quietly into a summer dusk.

BASHO'S ROBES

I am indeed dressed like a priest, but priest I am not,
for the dust of the world still clings to me.
— Matsuo Bashō

NOTES TOWARD MAKING

I.

The moment
revises itself
by angles,

torrential light
mingling loss,
rain

scores the wood
to woolen
moss—

and phonemes,
mercury nails
welling in buckets,

incite words
their agile
rebellions.

2.

The city aches into speech
of subway tunnels
and exit ramps.

Buses migrate over the rise
raveling lights
from this wet street,

to a tin
souvenir moon.
The hills billow

in a shirt of fog—
history
grinds out fictions,

brick
holds its wall.

3.

We unlock the piano

to lie on sound:
laundry mat, the cracked
stair,

a stop sign stolen,
every block
's an octave

in broken time,
no two things alike
but each rhymes with each.

4.

The rain as desire
fulfilled
by wind beating sideways

against glass,
revised to a new medium,
colorless, rinsed

flowers held up by no stem
among real cars
deliberate as murder,

a woman with one shoe
asleep
in the median.

5.

Bone fields and beating wind
thresh memory
thru black fire—

birds revolve
at the ends
of wire,

glittering turquoise plastics
of thought:
intersections crossed and stirred

by awkward
musics,
a dead leaf scra

tches the street.

6.

Life one
moment from now

flickers beneath this ice:
we break ourselves
toward it—a forest

of bone trees
stands in the eye's
declivities,

waving
as the night waves
of underwater fires.

HARTFORD STREET ELEGY

for Philip Whalen

you carry your body
                   bare feet
against the wood grain

         the bell   mute
             on its pillow

—❧—

         after meditation
in Langmusi   the monks
            tickle one another
tumble the temple steps
         laughing & kicking
            dragonflies
                at black noon
         dying casually
               over the lake

—❧—

a thousand years
of rain

in the wood grain
you carry your body

blessing the demons also
            that they might be freed
       from hell

the bell   silent on its pillow
continues to ring

a thousand years
                    ha!
in the wood grain
                    ha ha ha!

          take off yr shoes!

you carry your body

up
the narrow

stairs

breathing
as a bear breathes

          the robe
hung in crimson

          swings out
when you turn

1

ancient pond;
the frog jumps in—
splash!

2

a frog leaps
      into the old well—
sound of water

3

self absorbs
      into the flux
death bell or birth?

4

                pear rots
         in the entropy of bees
dark night of the soul

5

dragon in search of the golden sun ball
dives into a koan [old well: new water]
the myriad worlds

6

a thief plummets
from the fire escape:
listen

7

Grandpa mumbles
about the truck in snow
insinuating tomorrow

8

desire
occluded by the dream—
one feather dipped in blood

9

$y = mx + b$
$x^2 + y^2 = 169$
$\varnothing$

10

Quetzalcoatl
          disappears into capitol steps   :
history

11

twin snakes
          coupling in the garden
          dew on the jasmine

12

     thesis
antithesis
          synthesis

13

       Oedipus overlooks himself
in the sphinx
      unified in the oracle

14

the boy is older
     than his mother
shaking loose the wars

15

suicide note:
the world is a nothing
blooming

16

Krishna reaching out through everything
gives Radha a blue bracelet
we live by the sound of its rustling

17

no frog without
this rain: no rain
without this frog

18

servant girl wearing the king's medallion
falls into her own reflection
poetry

19

    iroko tree
    offers to a circle of young wives
    seed in the belly

20

    no target no
            arrow no bow
    bull's eye!

21

    man-lion at dusk
    Nara Singha—
            the gateless gate

22

all day rain falls
until mountains return to egg
in the whiteness

23

    bare arm
briefly lit against the night
then the banjo

24

ferry boat crosses
    the swollen river
      despite the cries of warning

25

where
was the sound
before the sound?

27

from her left breast
my mother
fed me language

26

despite the wind
smoke draws a line
straight up from the candle

28

    by use of transitional objects the infant
    actuates into the larger community
    but not without trauma

29

    minnows nibble
        roots in dark water
    the child is thinking

30

    the dancer
    dissolves into energy
    latent in the audience

31

    in the cage

                  he wakes
  beside his old harmonica

32

    Mt. Fuji

         floating
  on the eye

            makes a new thing
  not me: not snow

33

            the frog has escaped
  to lay her eggs

          in the rain gutter

ARC OF INTENTION

THE MILE

My grandmother crowns the hill,
her headlights lathing the dark,
a farm route

through rye then cotton
then the red and gold of wheat,
the scrub oak crowding

a little nameless river
where fog holds to low places.
Who would have seen the tractor

aimed down the highway by a boy—
his first summer behind the wheel
with no lights but the holy

somnolence of a cowboy radio?
The next car over the rise
is my father

blind into the fog.
There is so much to talk about
at this moment,

so many lines of cause and effect
trembling taut into that gully.
How does my father choose—

with his mother's ribs broken,
his new wife moaning from the ditch—
to carry the limp body

of someone else's child
a mile over night fields
toward the insinuation of a roof?

Everyone is bleeding and starlight
drizzles over the summer wheat.
The poem holds them there

long enough to trace the flight
of an owl
from a cedar's black minaret

its wings underlit by brake-lights.
Which of you, dear reader,
is in the next Oldsmobile

to clatter over the bluff
shouting *help* into your CB radio?
Which of you opens the front door

weeping
to wrap your unconscious boy
in quilts? Do you kill

the man
who carries him?
In most endings I am never

born. In most,
you buy my family's farm cheap
at auction. Who among you

is rushing the ambulance
past the county line at *mile 67*
when the tire blows? The story

moves through telephone wires
at the pitiless speed of rumor:
when my father reaches the house

with the boy expiring in his arms,
a white rectangle of light
and grief

sears his eyes forever.
In the cave of my mother's
body

I listen to the first fire.

PHOTOGRAPH

In the only photo of Grandpa Sweeney,
he is standing in some rectangle of summer
beside his immortal Chevrolet

under the windy brush strokes
of silos and crows,
an Oklahoma as thin as this page,

smiling proudly over three children
in black-and-white clothes
folded into the engine of a colorless sun.

Grandpa

was a farmer. He died doing it.
To this day I imagine him
harvesting the wheat in that Chevrolet

cutting across the fields in
geometric patterns,
in triangles, in circles,

trying to outwit death,

death which lives even in the seed,
tiny death
enthroned in the grain.

INHERITANCE

And when she could walk no farther
she fell between the tracks to give birth.
Not a boy but a tree

rooted to the spot and began to grow
so that by dawn it might be strong enough
to stop the train.

The myrtle wore a fine yellow ash.
Gravel carried there by lackeys
was enough earth,

star chatter sifting down into drifts
was enough light for me, drunk on placenta
and too young to understand the odds.

Wind shined out from the mountain.
Cities grew up to either side.
Mother was facing the wrong way

so I sprouted backwards
into time
where no train could harm us.

THE ARC OF INTENTION

San Francisco, poetry workshop with youth from Central America

The students bend their necks
over the reflective surface

of paper
fixing the light of their gaze

inward
where the pencil is a scorpion,

a storm,
a grove

of swaying orange trees.
Again the arc is in them,

overwhelming, precise—
they gather at high windows,

lean out to rooftops, freighters
on the bay—to name

this world with the awkward
words, the borrowed words,

yet they are naming,
and through the windows the city

rises to meet them:
fire escape, goldfinch,

plum blossom, crane—
they try on the new

syllables like oversized robes,
some soldier's lost boot.

In this way the words are tamed,
even loved,

and their faces wear the glow,
unmistakably,

of recognition:
the *seagull*'s bright

circle
repeated in tower glass

or *cirrus clouds*
wandering pine mountains,

unseen
until now—the word.

They delight here, emergent,
shiny as found medallions,

the family's lost heirloom
worn all the while round their neck

invisibly—
the word.

The way space contemplates
itself,

the way bamboo leans
over its ravine

balanced along its curve
into gravity,

everything is shaped by that leaning,
love and

resistance,
   the rapt

arc of intention.

CALIFORNIA

In the wisdom of the Spanish language,
moon is *luna*
and mole is *lunar.*

As a result the girls are proud
to point out their moles,
little brown moons.

I like this one on my cheek.
I have three on my neck,
like my mom has, night pearls.

Heat blurs the air over I-40 thru Mojave.
Kids are sniffing paint then fucking in ditches.
It's natural.

When it rains the squat trees
uproot and wash away.
I've learned to accept myself.

CLIMAX

Along the way the boat will pass
     a temple
          where steps reach all the way down

to the water
     and priests are disappearing
          washed clean of their goodness.

The river will oxbow
     beyond tamaracks
          beyond bluebirds suspended

in mobiles of sound.
     You will touch your legs
          where the socks marked you

with daylight—
     you will laugh or sleep
          cooling your wrists in the water.

The current will spin
     unexpectedly
          describing beneath its skin

the shapes of hipbones
     and sunken doors—
          when you are ready

you will release the oars
     and stand
          into the arc of the fall.

TREE

The jacaranda sways
in a great circle
and many smaller circles.

The purple blooms
have found their orbit
on this low hill.

Wind inside the
leaves
keeps them turning

on a still day.
That's how I love
Jennifer.

I think toward her.

KOCHANEK

Meeting Jennifer's family, Tolland, Connecticut

We are gathered
in these rooms of words, leaning in
clumsily

around a pinball machine, each
unknown
to himself. Lights

jangle and bang the numbers
round the happy wheels, a laughing
urgent search

for what this family
in a year or one single
hour

lost.
A man
carries on his shoulders his own

bewildered boyhood,
looking on,
attentive and afraid—he must

somehow learn what the others
know already.
The signs float by in-

decipherably. Would you like a cup
of tea, some coffee, the morning
paper? Whatever you do don't

read the front page.
Yes, sir, thank you, sir,
no.

A man
goes to meet himself
in rooms opening unexpectedly

round a corner
where a wall had been and down
a flight of stairs.

Sweep
the spiders from the cracks,
bake the pies,

we'll clean the glass doors together.
Of course, sir, yes, I'd like that.
Between us

a plane of dirty glass
to wash
incessantly

if we'll be understood: I
on the inside and you
on the outside—

speaking
out of a dazed silence,
this language

borrowed but never
owned,
never fully lived in.

In rooms known and unknown
I rise in the night and go
to meet myself, blinking

in mad love
and terror,
I outside and you inside

the house.
I folded her laundry today.
The shirts and dresses

still held her,
still sheltered her thin arms.
Shaken

by more love than I knew
existed, I wept
and feared

at my back her father
might catch me
with the lacy bra

in my hands. *Dirty*
orphan, get out!
The grass is cut,

deck swept,
lawn table encircled with chairs
hauled up from the basement,

ready for tomorrow: firmly
seated with apparitions
of future possibility. The aunts

lie dreaming in other houses,
uninvented, unborn
at this hour, languishing

in the rooms of sleep,
where the numbers on the doors
rearrange or disappear—

in deep woods,
gauzed in a blue ground fog,
the trees all hung with bells,

goat-footed elves
gather for the wedding
of the one indivisible

self—night eternally suspended
before tomorrow stumbles
across the threshold of a blue door,

the blue of Polish glass,
of bridges refracted on the points
of water, unworldly blue

of the artist,
unconscious but irrepressible—
where at last I find the man,

the second father.
I will marry this woman,
snow owl and wolf and

eyes flickering from underwater caverns.
May I never know her entirely,
may her migrations elude me,

the seasons that bronze and cast her
uncut forests into a white
effulgence. This is her house—

her language that I
sit folding
on the living room floor

while her family flashes and rings
around the pinball—
tomorrow, invite me!

Curtain behind curtain
releases,
the guests float in beds

toward the hour of coffee:
the days are docks to row
toward, swim toward,

step onto blindly, then
shake off sleep with the pass of a razor,
the knotting of a tie.

In a dream called tomorrow
the cats
are gathering to be fed:

Mother climbs the spiral well, calling
their animal names
in mellifluous and windy

vowels. The house—
shifting planes, invented
out of an inexhaustible

source—has no
limits!
We meet ourselves

unexpectedly in far kitchens,
the tea party, the piano lesson,
hands full of clues, sand

from the docks
on our feet
tracked upstairs, the sea's

voices call
from a lower room
(misunderstood)

moon-drenched halls, towers,
eclipses
where the self stood in the way

of light.
Songs buried
by the back porch, inviolate as bone,

beg
for the lost summer
hour when the woods began

to gray.
I will marry
your daughter. I am she already.

I give
birth
to myself

looking out the window at the badminton
net!
In a word alone

are many rooms:
Trementozzi,
McSweeney, Bruins, Kochanek:

In the mouth of war
Jennifer's grandmother,
little Viola, learned to sing,

to wash men's clothes
and share a bathroom
with all of Europe's

exiled tribes—
quarrels in the kitchen,
strikes at the fabric mill,

the Polish cadence,
Hungarian, Portuguese,
fricative, sibilant, under-

currents of the mother river—
we all
live in that house.

One night is too brief
to understand it.
Dawn wet in the pine,

the finches sing from their thicket.
I rise to meet
my new family.

NOTES

The Navajo Poet: Flint Wing is a trickster god of the four-state area (New Mexico, Arizona, Colorado, Utah). During the first period after the Creation, when gods walked among people in the original city, the people conspired to overthrow the gods. Flint Wing, feigning sleep, kept one eye open to spy on the prideful conspiracy, then flew up to tell the gods of the betrayal. The gods destroyed the city and scattered the tribes in all directions. Simon Ortiz, the Laguna Pueblo poet, told me this story at dawn in his adobe-style home outside of Acoma, New Mexico, the oldest inhabited city in North America. Flint Wing and Simon's new turquoise Pontiac appear in the poem. Fifteen years later, in 2004, Sherwin Bitsui, a young Navajo poet of the White Goat Clan of Northern Arizona, visited San Francisco, and I was moved by his poetry and what it heralded—a new generation of Native poets.

Bear: The Iroquois Mohawk poet, Maurice Kenny, was my teacher at the University of Oklahoma, and my inspiration to become a poet. "Cabala," distinct from the Hebrew "Kabbalah," is a term derived from the Latin, caballus, for horse, and signifies the universal "unspoken language," easily understood by all according to Fulcanalli, and which Cyrano de Bergerac calls "the instinct or voice of nature." According to Philip Lamantia, in his notes in *Becoming Visible* (City Lights, 1981), "The figurative image of the cabala as spiritual vehicle is the Pegasus of the Hellenic poets and derives from the Greek word for source.

Translation: My father and I traveled to Israel and Palestine in 1997. I wrote the first notes for this poem in the impoverished Palestinian town of Bethlehem.

Methodist: My maternal grandfather, Leslie Dale Smith, was a revered Methodist minister. I grew up attending his sermons in Dale, Oklahoma.

Oklahoma: My grandmother, Lucille, was part Cherokee and lived in western Oklahoma. When she told owl or bear stories to my sister and me, her voice tones and imagination were mesmerizing.

The Great Poems: In his essay, "Imagination as Value," Wallace Stevens wrote, "The great poems of heaven and hell have been written and the great poem of the earth remains to be written."

Hartford Street Elegy: This poem is an elegy for Philip Whalen, marking the last moment I saw him alive, climbing the stairs of the Hartford Street Zendo (in San Francisco) toward his private room. The quote in italics is from his poem, "The Bay Trees Were About to Bloom" in the book, *Overtime.* Langmusi is a Tibetan temple city in Szeshuan. During my travels through western China, on several occasions I experienced Tibetan monks to be as playful and joyous as they were devout and contemplative.

33 Translations of One Basho:
10: Quetzelcoatl is the legendary snake bird or feathered serpent, an Aztec god of the sky and Creation.

19: The iroko tree at the heart of the Yoruban Sacred Grove figures prominently in West African legend, as a bringer of abundance and fertility, as well as mischief (in cases where an ogre inhabits the tree). In one village, after a long period without babies being born, women gave sacrifice to the iroko ogre in order to become fertile again, careful to keep their backs to his tree as his gaze was deadly.

21: An East Indian demon could not be killed by man or animal, human or god, inside or outside, during the day or the night. Nara

Singha was the man-lion, the fourth incarnation of the Hindu God, Vishnu. He killed the demon at dusk on the threshold to his house, acting as neither man nor animal, and neither god nor human. In this way Vishnu triumphed over the illusion of duality.

27: Jacques Lacan developed the theory that language, the milk of culture, is fed to the human baby by the mother.

Inheritance: My Irish ancestors helped build the railroads west, before settling on farms in Oklahoma. They are the "lackeys" in the poem.

The Arc of Intention: I taught poetry workshops in the San Francisco WritersCorps for seven years. Most of my students were newly arrived teenagers from Central America, China, and the Middle East. They attended Mission High School, one block away from the original San Francisco Mission. The students wrote poetry and learned English at the same time, while trying to make a home of this new city.

Kochanek: I wrote this poem between 4 and 6 a.m. during the summer of 2000, a few hours before I would meet my fiancée Jennifer's extended family of Kochaneks and Trementozzis—grandparents, aunts, uncles, and siblings—who were gathering for a feast to celebrate our engagement.

ABOUT THE AUTHOR

Chad Sweeney was born in Norman, Oklahoma. He is the author of *An Architecture* (BlazeVOX, 2007) and *A Mirror to Shatter the Hammer* (Tarpaulin Sky, 2006). His poems and translations have appeared widely, including in *Best American Poetry 2008.* He edits *Parthenon West Review* with David Holler, and is the editor of *Days I Moved Through Ordinary Sounds* (City Lights, 2009), an anthology of poetry, fiction and memoir by the teaching artists of the national WritersCorps. With Mojdeh Marashi, Sweeney translated a book of Iranian poetry, *Arghavaan, Selected Poems of H.E. Sayeh,* for which he was awarded a grant from the San Francisco Arts Commission. He earned a B.A. in English from the University of Oklahoma and an MFA in poetry from San Francisco State University. He is currently a Ph.D. candidate in literature/poetry at Western Michigan University, where he teaches creative writing and serves as assistant editor for New Issues Press. He lives in Kalamazoo with his wife, poet Jennifer Kochanek Sweeney.